T0199184

GEMMALISA'S *Journey*

From Orphan with Cleft Lip and Palate to Adopted and Repaired

C. J. EMERSON

WestBow Press books may be ordered through booksellers or by contacting:

WestBow Press
A Division of Thomas Nelson & Zondervan
1663 Liberty Drive
Bloomington, IN 47403
www.westbowpress.com
1 (866) 928-1240

ISBN: 978-1-9736-5789-7 (sc)
ISBN: 978-1-9736-5790-3 (e)

Library of Congress Control Number: 2019903403

Print information available on the last page.

WestBow Press rev. date: 3/22/2019

WESTBOW
PRESS®
A DIVISION OF THOMAS NELSON
& ZONDERVAN

This is dedicated to my princess, Gem. She is the bravest person I know. Her love and care for others shines through her very being, and we are blessed to be called her family and friends. She is the angel who lives among us. I love you with all my being. Go on to continue to touch others by your story.

And to her prince, John Mulliken, MD, whose expertise in plastic surgery at Boston Children's Hospital gave her beauty upon beauty.

CHAPTER 1

The Seed of a Dream

Once upon a time, there was the tiniest, littlest black-haired baby girl born in a country far away on a day and time that only one person—or possibly two—knew about. They stared into her fragile face, and their hearts filled with fear, worry, and wonder of what to do next. A gaping hole filled the top of the inside of her mouth and left a long, open slit on both sides of her top lip. What to do? What to do? A beautiful, delicate, little girl needed so much care and so much medical surgery. They had a mix of throbbing emotions of wanting to hold and nurture the little baby while knowing she must be given away for her to have all that she required to live a better life.

A loving, agonizing, tearful decision was made to hide her where she could readily be found. The only hope was for someone to take her and provide for her the expensive care that was an absolute must. So this little bundle was wrapped tightly in layers of clothes, kissed, sobbed over, and left beside a busy road for someone to hopefully find sooner than later.

A passerby, who may have found others before this one, heard the lonely, sad wail of a child begging someone to find her and hold her and feed her. Feed her? How? There was no upper lip to suckle a bottle. A cavernous hole barricaded the proper way for food to go where it naturally went when swallowed. She was swiftly and carefully scooped up and taken to the police for proper placement and immediate nourishment. Due to her unique situation, she was most likely transferred quickly to the local orphanage, where many little girls with no known homes were laid in a small bed, often with others for warmth. There, caretakers needed to problem-solve how to feed a starving child with or without mouth deformities. This child was different. This petite little girl could not suckle a bottle or be left to feed herself in anyway. She needed to be held and spoon-fed formula with the notation in her first historical records that she was most likely only one day old.

One day old and already whisked from her mother and into the arms of several unfamiliar people, so her anxiety increased.

The prompting to eat began, and this rush of liquid frightened her. She gagged, so her caretaker stayed patient and gently coaxed her into eating enough to remain alive. She was so tiny and so pale, but her eyes were as bright as the starlight and had the darkest sparkle pulling you toward her, enticing you to get to know her. She seemed to gaze right through you, and in some way, she understood that her situation was dire and there was a great question of whether she would actually live. This caretaker saw her fears and was in tune with her little whimpers. This caretaker made it her mission that this one would survive and would go on to live a good life.

For this baby, her hands became her toys as she lay in her bed possibly next to another—but possibly not because her condition was seen by some as a curse, meaning none should look at her or be with her. Her caretaker did not believe this and provided companionship to keep her eating and surviving. Maybe she sang or hummed to her because this child loves music and singing. Maybe she told her stories because this wee one loved to see, hear, and listen to story after story. Maybe she held her hand, because this child desired touch only from those few people she truly trusted. This child learned quickly at night when it got dark that no attention could be given, no matter how loud they wailed, because all needs had been met and all babies had to get their necessary sleep. So all became eerily quiet until morning light finally came exploding and the hustle and bustle of stirring, hungry babies looked for the bottle of nourishment or the prepared food that came at only certain times.

This baby girl desired to shed her blankets and clothing, but due to her being so small, she was kept covered to make sure she was warm and snug. Her caretaker lifted her up and held her tight as she spoon-fed formula and congee despite the loud, forceful objection that was spewed out of this unhappy little one's wide-open mouth, because to not eat meant sure death. The slow-growing baby was full of life and longed to live. She was stubborn beyond belief and would fight being fed as much as she fought to live. The only thing in her favor was that her very own caretaker was as focused on staying the course and determined as this little ball of fire was. Failure was not an option because to fail meant to lose face to dishonor oneself. This caretaker would not let this child die, no matter what. The child was placed back into her bed because there was no other place for her to go. All she could do all day was stare above because she was too weak and could not turn over.

Day after day, time after time, the same routine was faced. Day after day, her hair started to wear away in the back of her head until she was hairless. She memorized what she saw and once again used only her hands to move in front of her as a distraction from the monotony of everyday sameness with nothing to stimulate the brain to think beyond only her imagination. The sounds of others were beginning to not be heard as fluid started building in each ear due to no drainage because her birth disability caused her to become clinically deaf. She saw lips move but did not hear one word spoken. Vision became the primary sensory organ, and she noticed every little move. Touch became essential in sensing that she mattered to at least one person. The name Ning Cai Ling was given, with the caretaker feeling proud that her own name was included in hers. Though many looked upon her and saw ugliness, turning their faces away so as to not see her, this child was beautiful both inside and out. She wanted to live as she slowly gained weight one begrudging ounce at a time.

Other babies moved on to putting solid food in their mouths by using their gums to feel it and gnaw on it—apples, crackers, bread, etc.—but not this baby. Food was a feared object. A fear of dying, of choking, of knowing that whatever was put in her mouth did not feel right inside a gaping hole and hurt. Food was fought. Food was forced, and screaming at mealtime continued. Every feeding time was anticipated with the rise of anxiety to the point that it could be seen in her eyes, heard in her voice, and her body trembled at the thought of any food except liquid being placed in her mouth. No surgery could be done until she weighed twenty pounds or more, so the caretaker stayed true to her little feisty one and fed despite the opposition and unhappiness. The caretaker braced herself for the battle that came at every meal time. Older children in the orphanage milled around to help to try to comfort Ling Ling, as she is called, but no comfort came at mealtimes—only sheer terror. To give her what she wanted meant sure end of life as her nutritional needs grew with her age.

Her weakness kept her from turning, sitting, or walking, and she did not progress as others. She only lay in her bed while looking above and watching as her hands swung from side to side in front of her. Her only control was how fast or slow she moved them. Little Ling Ling remained not hearing as fluid stayed bottled up in both ear canals, the secondary issues related to cleft lip and palate. She did not speak but sobbed, unless she laughed when her hands did something that she thought was funny. Oh Ling Ling, your God-chosen mother did not know that you existed. She only knew she was coming for another child who was matched to her and waited for her. The caretaker thought, Please choose life, beautiful miracle baby who knows not that another mother is coming. This mother knew not that you would be her most precious gift.

CHAPTER 2

Germination of a Dream

Ling Ling's mother to be was on the older side of life and lived on the opposite side of the world. Being the oldest of ten children growing up gave her much experience of crying babies around. She chose to never marry because the "right" person had not come along, but she chose a profession of helping others in teaching and counseling. Her best friend, a nurse of more than twenty years, had taken her on a long journey to a foreign land two years prior to help her and her husband adopt their fifth child, the second from this beautiful country. This mother to be fell in love with this little new girl and wished for one of her own. Fourteen-month-old Lilani was like the mother's own, even though Lilani's names for the mother to be was Ninny and then Auntie. Lilani would soon have a "younger sister" who would change her world from the youngest to the next to the youngest. And the new one would challenge her in how to help and relate to a child who even the mother did not know was to come.

One day this mother soon to be saw a three-year-old child on the adoption waiting list and knew that that child was to be her child. She would trade in all her worldly possessions, including her retirement, and seek her brother and sister-in-law's financial help to get her new daughter. Her best friend also sacrificed in obtaining the funds to once again, for the third time, go get a precious child to bring back to America and give her a forever home. The adoption agency here and abroad became the guides, cheerleaders, and comforters and provided the ultimate sacrifices in making sure the precious children from foreign lands were matched correctly and provided with all that was required to be successful in a forever-loving home.

The long, exhausting plane trip was filled with mixed emotions and wonderings of how this older child would accept a new mother, how she would be with someone who did not know her native language, and how she would adjust coming from an orphanage that she had lived in her whole early life. This mother had attended all the classes about foreign adoption and read books upon books that explained the difficulties of adopting an older child. So the fears were real.

Too real, as she was about to experience.

CHAPTER 3

The Dream Enters

The large three- to four-year-old child entered the government room quietly and in a very shy manner. She accepted the nearing approach of complete strangers cautiously, and she was exactly as pictured. The adoption agency guide was a very kind man who made sure that everything was going as planned and remained available twenty-four hours per day as the first twenty-four hours were the test of whether the child would be adopted fully or not. This child was full of energy and excited about the outside world, especially the new foods of the hotel. She loved watermelon and could not seem to get enough of it. She stayed close by, hesitant at times of what she could do or not do. She struggled with sleep in an unfamiliar place with a foreign new mother whom she had previously seen only in a picture given to her by the orphanage caretakers. They had obviously coached her on what to say and do, yet in full native language, not English. The wonderful guide acted as the humble translator.

After her first night and a time viewing the native culture, the mother proceeded with signing the adoption papers to become the mother of a three-year-old child she barely knew. Almost immediately after that agreement, the child decided she was not sure of this match and became quite outwardly oppositional. For the single mom, it was far too concerning to think that she could parent her alone, but she did not want to dishonor her in this story by being specific about these difficulties.

She spoke to her guide and told him of the many worries and the need to reevaluate this decision for this child. He made some phone calls and found that not all her information had been readily shared (probably fearing she would not be adopted) with the agency. It was decided together that it was far more acceptable according to the native customs and care for those in orphanages for her to be raised there in her own culture and not in a faraway country. This child had decided that America was not her country and maybe, just maybe, another family could take on this special child and give her a forever family in her home country.

The mother said her teary goodbyes, and the guide took the child back to the orphanage. The mother gave her all she and her friend had brought and bought as far as physical things of clothes. Then the mother wished her a good life in her home country, where she could be free to express herself and would be more accepted. The mother's heart and inner being were in a state of shock. She had come all this way and had no child. All this way to decide the only child she came for needed to stay right there, and the kind caring guide agreed. She felt so sick inside, yet she knew the child she came for was really bonded with her own people. To take her would have been not in the best interest of her not-to-be daughter. But for her to go back home with no child felt like failure and guilt.

CHAPTER 4

The Stop of a Dream

The mother had resigned herself that she was traveling home with much money spent and no child to raise. But an inner peace prevailed that the little girl was where she needed to be. It took the government to make the adoption null and void, and the guide took care of all this. In the eyes of the law of the land, the child had no mother and the mother had no daughter. But in the hearts of both, they knew and wept for the loss.

CHAPTER 5

The Shock of a New Dream (It Is Still Happening)

The mother's loving, kind, best friend prayed that she would have an open heart and encouraged her to allow herself to be rematched to another child. They had come to receive a special needs child, so they asked for another child to be presented. The guide took her to yet another government building, where the legal adoption of one child was dissolved and the process of another was initiated. Again, all this was conducted in the native language with her friend, and she was patiently awaiting the outcome and looking for direction of what to do next. A few children in that area were mentioned, but none matched her ability to parent. They left on yet another plane to see what might be found in the city where the government agency that finalized the medical part of all adoptions resided. There they were presented with three children with very special needs.

The mother's greatest dread, due to not having any prior experience, was to parent a child with cleft lip and palate. But the little girl presented and chosen had severe cleft lip and palate and was a mere fifteen months old. Just a baby with a wide-open face. No pictures or any other information was provided. The mother agreed and proceeded on to her next unknown journey of being "foreign government wisdom matched" with the most precious gift that God could ever provide.

The adoption agency at home and in the foreign land coordinated quickly to provide all the paperwork the government needed for the switch to this new teeny, tiny girlie. They had no diapers, bottles, clothes, or toys—absolutely nothing for a little baby. All that they had was sent with her three-year-old. It was off to Walmart in a foreign land, where it truly had all that was needed plus some extras. And the adoption agency supplied everything it could due to donations at its building. It was God at work, supplying needs right before their eyes. A blessing to the mother was her nurse friend of so many years loved buying baby clothes and picking out what was needed. The mother was still in a daze and trying to wrap her head and heart around a new baby. Their budget was blown, and they now had to live on little or nothing for the next few weeks of tuna sandwiches and ramen noodle soup in a bowl.

Their little two-year-old Lilani was home with the mother's brother and sister-in-law and spread around to other family members and was in much need of seeing her mother and auntie. She was going to be surprised to get a little baby to hold! The mother and her friend felt torn, but grateful, that they had such a loving family who would be waiting in the United States of America for a new one to attach to them as her forever family. Chinese people talk about a red thread that connects the hearts of those meant to be together. This red thread was beginning to weave and wind tightly as the anticipation of actually meeting the new daughter was happening in a rapid pace. The mother to be was trying to somehow get word to the other side of the world that the plans had all changed and they had to stay longer.

That night, they needed a new name. The other little child had hers, but now they had a new one and she needed her own special name to set her apart. So Gemmalisa was chosen as a gem and to hold a name that combined much love for her.

CHAPTER 6

The Surprise of a New Dream

The new day finally dawned to get the highly anticipated bundle. Little did they know that her initial medical information was not correct.

They were taxied to the new government building with new guides because they had to say goodbye in the other province to their first guide, whom they would never forget. As they sat down, a document was placed before them with the picture of a tiny baby with her premaxilla protruding from her wide-open bilateral mouth that basically showed she did not have a nose. It did seem like love at first sight. It also gave her birth date with the year 2005, identifying her as thirteen months and not fifteen months. Her eyes were the brightest, shiniest eyes they had ever seen and drew them in like a south pole to a north pole magnet. They were stuck, never to let go. None of the gorgeous baby's disabilities mattered to them at that time, only getting their hands on her. Her medical record was limited, and no other information was offered, only that she weighed 16.8 pounds at thirteen months old. She was a small, tiny precious baby.

The magical moment had arrived as they heard someone come in the outer door and some conversation was exchanged in the native tongue. They had no clue what was being said, and there was no interpreter because the new guide was outside the door. They only knew that their life was about to change into something they had never dreamed would happen. This would be the first time the woman—at age forty-six—would be mom to the most loving, gentle, precious, little orphan girl who soon would not be an orphan. The little girl was an angel who was to bless her and her family beyond belief.

Ning Cai Ling was carried into the large multiseated room by her very own one-on-one caretaker and orphanage director. She was so very tiny to look at with nothing but her orphanage clothes and the fancy orphanage book that was presented to the mother due to her paying the orphanage fee. Little Ling Ling, soon to be Gemmalisa, was finally placed in her mother's arms. And as she was lifted up, she stared with those bright, beautiful eyes and smiled the widest, most open-mouthed smile as she grabbed the front of her new mother's shirt so tightly as if to say, "This is my momma, and I am never ever letting go!"

The mother was in pure love with a baby she had no time with but wanted to share the rest of her life breaths loving and protecting. Her daughter. Her child. Her Gemmie. It was commitment for life in that first moment. Yes, she wanted her. Yes, she would take her and adopt her. Yes, she would parent her. Yes, she could parent her. Yes, no matter what it took and no matter how much money, she would be a faithful, kind mother until death do they part.

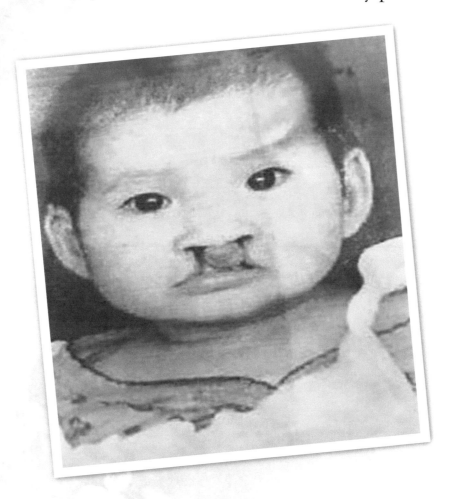

The first day of trying to feed their precious baby was one of sheer torture for both. The nurse buddy took over and the mother was relieved to hold, stroll around, change, but not feed. The wonderful nurse friend took on the task of figuring out how in the world to get food into a mouth so open with a baby fighting and screaming.

God had the answer to prayer just across the street. They came across some bottles that had a spoon attached to where the nipple would be, and it allowed food to drip down and onto the spoon placed in the mouth. This became Gemmalisa's new happy way of finally feeling comfortable with formula being administered slowly and at her pace.

Little did the mother know at that time that her Gem would become very locked in her thinking of how something should be.

CHAPTER 7

The Perfection of an Amazing Dream

They had to return the next day to the very same governmental building to officially sign the adoption papers. Her caretaker was anxious to see her again, but Ning Cai Ling had become Gemmalisa overnight and clung relentlessly to her mother with no intention of ever going back to her caretaker. Her caretaker smiled and out of sheer politeness stated that Gemmalisa had her mother's complexion. The mother thanked her and signed her life to Gemma's life, never to look back or regret regardless of how hard the road to help her would be.

There were difficult evaluations and surgery at Boston's Children's Hospital with Prince John Mulliken, MD, performing intricate miracles to her palate and lips. Later, his protégé, Dr. Padwa, took bone from her hip and put it in her palate for strength and true closure. Many ear, nose, and throat doctors helped her to become fully hearing again. And her pediatricians lovingly helped her due to her anxiety around medical people and ongoing ear infections that stopped when surgery solved it all.

Gemma's journey to home—her true American home—had begun. Her native land will always be a part of her, including the caring, loving people who took care of her in her most desperate of situations. But a forever family that adores her and remains her loyal companions remain to this day and forever more.

Gemmalisa still faces obstacles every day due to more medical issues, but this is a story to come later. Stay tuned.

This is not the end!

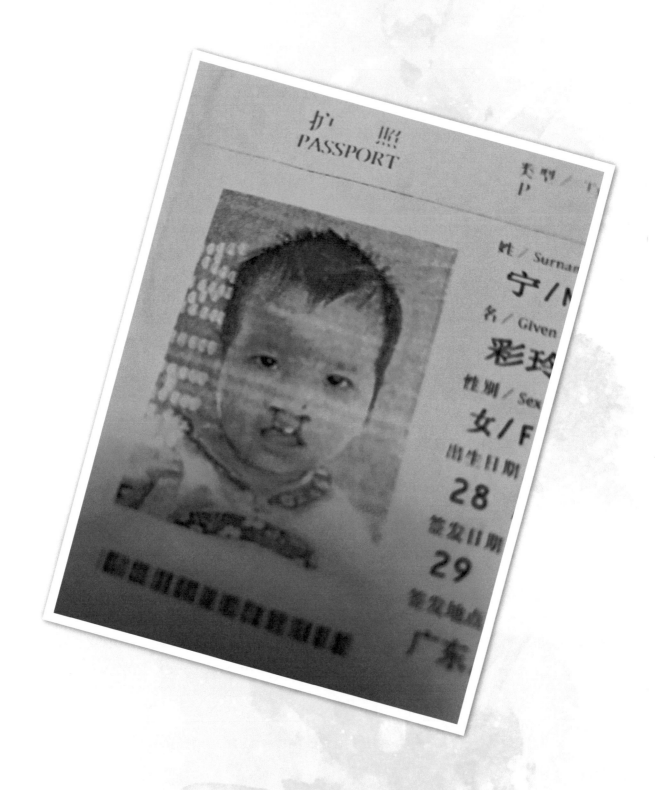

Printed in the United States
By Bookmasters